THE DISEASE OF ADDICTION

A TWENTY-FIRST CENTURY UNDERSTANDING AND BEYOND

JOSEPH CARAVELLA, MA, LADC

This book is not intended as a substitute for the medical advice of physicians. The reader should regularly consult a physician in matters relating to their health and particularly with respect to any symptoms that may require diagnosis or medical attention.

The Disease of Addiction: A Twenty-First Century Understanding and Beyond ©2019
By Joseph Caravella
ISBN: 978-1-7331107-2-3

Left foot in
for those left out.

CONTENTS

Preface

My path to recovery began in 2008. A more formal study of addiction began three years later. After countless hours of empirical observation, participation in over a thousand twelve-step meetings, obtaining a graduate degree, and years treating the illness, it is apparent that addiction is not an easy subject to understand. However, knowledge is power! After a close study of the best textbooks and reports elucidating the biology of addiction, I believe the information is sound and of the utmost importance. The challenge, then, lies in explaining a complex brain disease to a person with a dysregulated brain. Not to mention worried family members and loved ones and all the persons in our society who still believe addiction is a matter of choice.

It has been my privilege to lecture on the disease of addiction to large treatment populations for years. Inspired by requests for written material beyond my lectures and on a personal mission to improve addiction education, I wrote this short book as a meditation exploring the evolutionary perspective of chemical use, the origins of the Alcoholics Anonymous program, current understanding of the neuroscience of addiction, and how scientific evidence substantiates the Twelve-Step solution.

I speak directly to the person struggling with their chemical use who is ambivalent about change. In my eyes, they are the newcomer to recovery. And when discussing addiction, they are the sort for whom I am most concerned.

Special thanks to my clients, mentors, colleagues, family, friends, and especially my wife for supporting this effort. I have learned many recovery lessons over the years. Here's an important one: I can only keep what peace and love I have by freely giving it away.

In part, this is my love for you.

A HISTORICAL PERSPECTIVE OF CHEMICAL USE

"The vine bears three kinds of grapes: the first of pleasure, the second of intoxication, the third of disgust."

—Diogenes

According to the available evidence and our best estimates, humans have been growing, cultivating, and experimenting with mood-altering chemicals for 10,000 years. Why? To cope with our environment and enhance our existence. Opium, alcohol, and cannabis for the purposes of relieving pain and "curing" many ailments. Alcohol, also referred to as *spirits*, for connecting with God, communing with one's tribe, and engaging in all kinds of spiritual expression. Hallucinogens have been used for similar purposes. It is worth mentioning that the cause of altered states of consciousness is not limited to chemicals; they can also occur secondary to compulsive behavior or mental illness.

It is an important distinction that the ways in which humans experience a chemical (intoxication) and to what degree (threshold) have changed drastically in the past 300 years. Technological advances in the synthesizing, refining, and manufacturing of chemicals have increased their potency to levels many times more powerful than other areas of human experience—like exercise, food, and sex. The development of faster and more efficient methods of delivering chemicals into the body—smoking, insufflation, and intravenous injection—has intensified their effects even more. Below is a selection of chemicals and the (recent!) year of their development on an evolutionary scale of 300,000 years for Homo sapiens:

Mass production of liquor in London (1710)
Inhalants: nitrous oxide, chloroform, and ether (1730)
Morphine refined from opium (1804)
Hypodermic needle (1855)
Cocaine refined from coca leaf (1859)
Heroin refined from morphine (1874)
Automatic cigarette rolling machine (1884)
Amphetamine (1887)
MDMA (1912)
Oxycodone (1916)
Methamphetamine (1919)
LSD (1938)
Librium (1955)
Fentanyl (1959)

The evolution of alcohol and its use has occurred over thousands of years. However, industrial-level production of beer and liquor did not begin until the eighteenth century. Opium is a reddish-brown, bitter-tasting substance extracted from the opium poppy juice—which is not the most practical or enjoyable substance to ingest.[1] While chronic— or "long-term"—oral ingestion of opium can bring about physical dependence (tissue dependence in the brain) and possibly addiction. The pleasure or intoxication threshold is much lower than modern opiate use, such as smoking or insufflation of heroin, or intravenous injection of oxycodone. Opium smoking did not become common until 1520, which reinforces the notion that the way in which humans use chemicals has changed very recently on an evolutionary scale.

Another example is marijuana, which, until the latter part of the twentieth century, contained only about 1% tetrahydrocannabinol (THC). Because of the sinsemilla growing method developed in the 1970s, THC content currently averages 10% but can increase to 30% when the plant is grown hydroponically. Refined, even more, modern marijuana concentrates can have THC contents up to 80%-100%! Our ancestors used marijuana 5,000 years ago for burial, medicinal, or

---

[1] I don't know this from personal experience, but after reading the early nineteenth-century book "Confessions of an English Opium-Eater" by Thomas De Quincey, I know all I need to know, thank you very much.

even recreational purposes, but they weren't consuming the plant via *dabbing* (inhalation of vaporized marijuana concentrate). Those same ancestors were also using opium and alcohol for pain relief. Though, there was no chance of sophisticated surgery, in part, because modern chemicals—like propofol,[2] midazolam, barbiturates, and fentanyl— were not available to anesthetize the patient. (This being in addition to the other necessary medical technologies.) There's evidence that coca leaves were being consumed for medicinal, nutritional, and religious reasons as far back as 3,000 years ago. Nonetheless, those ancient peoples would be hard-pressed to envision the leaf refined into a white powder, cooked into "crack" rocks, and freebased by Richard Pryor to the extent it inspired a 151-proof rum shower and self-immolation.[3]

The Birth of Alcoholics Anonymous

Alcoholics Anonymous, founded in 1935, was not the first mutual-aid group for persons struggling with alcohol abuse. Other organizations include the Washingtonian Movement, the Keeley Leagues, and the Oxford Group. For historical context, the 1920s and '30s were an extremely challenging time to be an alcoholic. Treatment resources were scarce and only accessible to the affluent. The Great Depression and Prohibition were, to say the least, strains. Alcoholics Anonymous (A.A.), the program of one alcoholic helping another, was born of necessity when society and medical science failed to address the problem of addiction adequately.

The first seed of A.A. was planted in a wealthy businessman named Rowland H. Despite his significant personal achievements, Rowland found himself hopeless and completely out of control with his alcohol use. He went to Zurich, Switzerland, and sought the help of Dr. Carl Jung, who, at the time, was considered one of the best physicians in the world. Treatment concluded and appeared successful, but it was not long before Rowland relapsed. Discouraged, he reached out to Dr. Jung again, only to be told his problem was beyond the scope of current psychiatric treatment. Though, Jung also told him that he had

---

[2] The drug that killed Michael Jackson.
[3] https://www.washingtonexaminer.com/crime-history-richard-pryor-sets-self-on-fire.

seen several cases of a severely addicted person being cured through a religious or spiritual experience.

Inspired, Rowland and his quest for a spiritual experience led him to New York City where he joined the Oxford Group, a popular spiritual movement, created by Frank Buchman.[4] The Oxford Group promoted the idea that a movement of personal spiritual change could solve the world's problems. Rowland stayed sober through his involvement in the Oxford Group, which included regular meeting attendance, spiritual growth, and service to other addicted persons. At this same time, he learned an old friend of his, Ebby T., was about to be permanently committed to an asylum because of his alcohol use and related consequences. Rowland and several other Oxford Group members intervened, gaining his release from police custody on the condition, they took responsibility for his well-being. Moved by Rowland's story, Ebby quit drinking and became an active member of the Oxford Group.

Radiant with hope and goodwill from his experience, Ebby remembered an old classmate of his, one of the worst alcoholics he had ever known. He met with William Griffith Wilson at his home in New York City in November 1934. He testified to his transformation through Oxford Group participation, but Bill wasn't particularly interested—the religious overtones made him uncomfortable. The next month, Ebby, with several Oxford Group members, went to visit Bill. But the trip was spoiled by his admission to Towns Hospital, a popular "drying-out" facility in Manhattan. Two days into his stay[5] and facing his mortality, Bill experienced a powerful and ultimately life-changing spiritual experience. To paraphrase Bill's report of his experience: A divine presence revealed itself and graced him with peace. Thinking he had experienced a hallucination or was losing his grasp on reality, Bill requested counsel with his attending physician Dr. William Duncan Silkworth. Dr. Silkworth admitted the experience was not wholly explainable by medical science, but rather than dismissing the experience; he encouraged Bill *not* to discount what had happened to him.

During his stay at Towns, Ebby gave Bill a copy of William James' book "The Varieties of Religious Experience," hoping it would

---

[4] Though, it was finessed for treating the alcoholic by Dr. Sam Shoemaker.
[5] His fourth in less than twelve months!

provide insight into what had happened to him. Bill did find the book helpful, as it provided a framework for his experience: discovering great strength and peace through pain and surrender.[6] In addition to the spiritual awakening and James' writings, Dr. Silkworth frequently reminded Bill he had an "allergy," or *abnormal physical response*, to alcohol. As such, recovery would have to include complete abstinence from alcohol, lest he trigger the addictive cycle all over again.[7] Silkworth also lessened Bill's shame and guilt by establishing a biological basis for his disease; that his struggles with alcohol were not entirely attributable to a moral or personal failing, which was the ubiquitous sentiment at the time. Bill began attending Oxford Group meetings facilitated by Dr. Shoemaker and he began envisioning a movement that would recreate the impact that Silkworth and James had had on him. Over the next six months, Bill tried to help other alcoholics get sober, but he had no enduring success.

A professional opportunity brought Bill to Akron, Ohio, in May of 1935.[8] But when the business meeting quickly fell apart, he found himself tempted to have a drink in the lounge of his hotel. Instead, Bill made a series of phone calls—seeking out another alcoholic to help—that resulted in an arranged meeting the next day between himself and Dr. Robert Holbrook Smith. Dr. Bob was approximately fifteen years older than Bill, nearly dead from his alcoholism, and less than inspired to meet with anyone to discuss his alcohol use; he suggested their meeting be limited to fifteen minutes. Nonetheless, the short meeting turned into hours of the men relating meaningfully about their trials and tribulations with alcohol—ruined professional careers, strained marriages and families, among other things. Bill enlightened Dr. Bob about the physical allergy to alcohol, the obsession of the mind, and the possibility of sobriety through spiritual change. In Dr. Bob's words, he had finally met someone who "knew what they were talking about when it came to alcohol." Dr. Bob took his last drink on June 10, 1935, and this would become the date formally recognized as the beginning of the Alcoholics Anonymous program. Bill moved to

---

[6] William James, a late nineteenth-century philosopher and scholar, is regarded as the father of American clinical psychology.

[7] If you're curious: Benjamin Rush, a late eighteenth-century physician, the father of American psychiatry, and a signatory of the *Declaration of Independence*, first posited alcoholism as an illness, or what he called a "palsy of the will."

[8] An executive position for a car tire manufacturer.

Akron that summer, residing with Dr. Bob and his wife Anne, and they began helping other alcoholics. There were many failures but several significant successes—enough to start a legacy of recovery in Akron. Bill moved back to Brooklyn, and with the assistance of his wife Lois, created a small group of recovering alcoholics using the approach started in Akron. This was the beginning of the most successful recovery program in American history. To this day other abstinence-based support groups are evaluated using A.A. as the standard of comparison. But in the early years of the program, A.A. didn't have an identity, let alone a concrete structure to help alcoholics. In essence, it was one person helping another, unconditionally.[9]

In 1935, the American health care system wanted nothing to do with alcoholics. A variety of reasons include: viewing them as moral degenerates; doctors misinterpreting physical withdrawal symptoms as "behavioral" problems; the population having a notorious nature for unsettled medical bills, plus high rates of readmission. To the credit and persistence of A.A. members, hospitals changed the way they viewed alcoholism—as an illness with a biological basis—and how they addressed the challenges of the disease, such as withdrawal syndrome, emotional instability, and social/economic insecurity. Hospitals and their ability to physically stabilize the individual in acute alcohol withdrawal would be crucial to the growth of Alcoholics Anonymous. As the program spread and matured in the 1940s and 50s, A.A. chose to discontinue, then avoid professional affiliation or endorsements of any kind. Rather, the organization would focus, with singleness of purpose, on helping other alcoholics. Accordingly, the very brief partnering of healthcare and Alcoholics Anonymous ended, and the beginning of a grossly insufficient effort by "modern" society to address addiction began.

Addiction in the Twenty-First Century

Why is exploring a historical perspective of chemicals and the history of A.A. helpful for understanding addiction in the twenty-first century? I will answer that question at length, but in short:

---

[9] The ancient Greeks referred to this inclusive love as *agape*. Agape is akin to *pure altruism* in philosophical jargon and *loving-kindness* in Buddhism.

- Pleasure and survival responses are the **same** in the brain.
- Mood-altering chemicals affect this region of the brain **100–1100%** more powerfully than naturally occurring pleasure responses.
- Acute and chronic intoxication can **subvert** the brain's natural survival mechanisms.
- A **permanent** change in brain structure results in a craving for using chemicals that supersedes even basic survival needs.
- While recovery is possible, the part of the brain that regulates its response to chemicals **never** resets or "heals" itself.
- Instead, continued chemical use perpetuates the change in brain structure, resulting in a more **powerful** craving.[10]

The Alcoholics Anonymous program defines addiction as having three distinct components: *the allergy of the body*, *the obsession of the mind*, and *the malady of the spirit*. The primary goal of this book is to demonstrate how science and modern understanding substantiate this framework for the disease.

In nature, rewards typically require time and effort. The use of mood-altering chemicals offers a heady shortcut. As a species, our brains have yet to adapt and, therefore, effectively process these potent dopaminergic responses. As evidenced by the fact that an estimated 10–12 percent of the United States population develops an abnormal response to chemicals, resulting in a substance use disorder or, less formally, "addiction." Additionally, many people struggle with other compulsions—such as gambling, pornography, overspending, or food—often with a similar scope of damage caused by addictions to chemicals. It should not be a surprise to learn that these behaviors affect the same part of the brain that mood-altering chemicals do. On an evolutionary scale of hundreds of thousands of years for our species, the advancements in chemicals are incredibly recent. With this knowledge in hand, maybe it is easier to understand—even from a bird's eye view—certain people in the general population having a

---

[10] Why addiction is a *progressive* illness.

greater sensitivity to, or being more inclined to have problems with their chemical use?

But maybe not.

Dr. Silkworth's hypothesis from the 1930s was that alcoholism is caused by an allergy of the body and fueled by an obsession of the mind. The founders of A.A. not only recognized the biological distinctions between themselves and the general population, they also suggested the maintenance of recovery would require lifelong effort in the realm of one's spiritual condition. I will also demonstrate how this "spiritual" component of recovery has a biological basis and is as vital as the abnormal response to chemicals and the many challenges that come with managing a chronic illness.

I concede the possibility that you have strong reservations or even preconceived notions about addiction as a disease, especially one equal to other illnesses like cancer or diabetes.

That's cool.

I'm also guessing you are an intelligent human being with tons of life experience and lessons learned, and perhaps even several academic degrees to boot. Still, if you are anything like me, when it comes to your relationship with chemicals, being too smart for your britches has not panned out one hundred percent in your favor. Then, to make matters worse, it is likely being suggested you reach out for and accept help from others with whom you may have nothing in common other than you all have issues with some form of chemical use. If I may suggest, please follow the evidence in a neutral and objective manner before coming to any significant, emotional conclusions. Maybe you approach this subject like an excellent research scientist or an investigative journalist would?

I admit that addiction has been poorly understood, much less treated, over time, and even today it remains shrouded in some level of mystery. I can't give you, the reader, an answer to the ultimate *why* as it pertains to addiction, but I aim to explain the *how* in an inclusive and easy-to-understand manner. Modern neuroscience and imaging techniques (PET and fMRI scans), beginning in the 1980s, have revolutionized and thoroughly substantiated addiction's legitimacy as a brain disease. Nevertheless, I am the first to agree that the delivery and spread of this scientific information in our current day and age range from spirited at best to grossly insufficient at worst.

Now, I am just stirring the pot, but riddle me this: Why is my friend, a neuroscientist who runs two laboratories at a respected university, searching for a cure for addiction if it is *not* a disease? I didn't say he is attempting to figure out whether addiction is an illness. I said he is looking for a *cure*. And if addiction is not a disease, do you think your insurer would be paying to treat it? Seriously, insurers do not pay for made-up diseases, or non-evidence-based treatment interventions, for that matter. I don't think of these points as smoking guns, but I implore you to ponder the answer to either—or both—of them.

Today, there are nonprofit, for-profit, state, and federal agencies dedicated to the treatment of addiction. However, medicine and its practitioners remain unprepared to address the full scope of the disease.[11] Addiction has been formally recognized as an illness by the American Medical Association and the American Psychological Association since the 1960s. But the underpinnings of the disease were not well understood until the past couple of decades. And while the medical world does not deny addiction's validity as an illness, it has yet to adjust its curriculums and residencies to account for the disease.[12] A recent study found that new physicians graduating from medical school had received, on average, only two hours of addiction-related education.[13] Then there are the disparities in addicted persons receiving professional help—only 10-15% of people struggling with chemical abuse will receive some form of professional services this year.

Moreover, while insurers offer chemical health benefits, they are second to mental health coverage, which is typically poorly covered and reimbursed. To make matters worse, a number of predatory wolves in healthcare clothing will cause direct harm to addicted persons by exploiting them for insurance fraud. Stigmatized illnesses and conditions have historically been ripe for abuse while also ignored by insurers and legislators.

All considered one can quickly become discouraged or even overwhelmed when examining the challenges facing addicted

---

[11] Addiction is causal for seventy-two other medical illnesses.

[12] Only 15 of 180 American programs currently teach that addiction includes alcohol, nicotine, and other drugs.

[13] For comparison, I received 1800 hours of training before I began practicing as a therapist.

populations. On a positive note, there are approximately twenty-three to twenty-five million individuals in recovery from addiction in this country right now. Statistically, most people who struggle with their chemical use and related issues will moderate or discontinue their use *without* traditional residential or outpatient services. That said, many will require professional intervention to help initiate recovery, with "early remission" being the first goal and "sustained remission" thereafter. The way providers diagnose addiction improved in 2013 when the DSM-5[14] redesignated addiction as a "substance use disorder"[15] with specifiers: mild, moderate, or severe. The specifiers improve clarity of symptom severity and thus treatment recommendations. There are many noble institutions and dedicated clinicians using evidence-based practices to treat persons holistically and with dignity and respect. And while societal changes will be slow—as they typically are—we can remember that the true spirit and ability to address addiction started with one individual helping another.

---

[14] *Diagnostic and Statistical Manual of Mental Disorders, 5th Edition.*
[15] Formerly known as *chemical dependency*.

THE ALLERGY OF THE BODY

"Look at situations from all angles, and you will become more open."

—Dalai Lama

Approximately 250-300 million years ago marked the beginning of the limbic system, sometimes referred to as the "mammalian" or "survival" brain. This region of the brain continues to promote and drive survival in our species today, and it has three main functions:

- Regulating physiological functions in the body: respiration, heartbeat, body temperature, hormone release.
- Mediating basic emotions and cravings: anger, fear, hunger, thirst, anxiety, pain, pleasure.
- Imprinting survival memories: a sound signifies danger, food taste good, sex produces more tribe members.

It may have stood out to you that cravings are a normal physiological process. For some time after I entered recovery, the word "craving" brought to mind vivid memories of using alcohol, heroin, or cocaine. It meant an incredible and uncompromising urge to use chemicals, no matter the cost. Therefore, it was a surprise to me when I learned its other meaning.

When a deer hears a twig snap in the woods, the limbic system responds *danger*, then, if needed, *spring* into action. When your mouth becomes dry, your limbic system responds *I am thirsty*. So, you get something to drink. The limbic system is also responsible for the fight-flight-freeze response, which I will explain through a totally not-made-up story:

I lived two miles from Hazelden's campus in Center City, Minnesota, during graduate school. And I can tell you. There are bears in them thar woods! Now imagine I'm out for a stroll in the woods surrounding Hazelden, and I run into a bear. Instantly, my limbic system kicks into gear, and the fight-flight-freeze response takes control of the thinking and insight-oriented part of my brain. The limbic system is actually four to five times faster and stronger than the neocortex, which is ideal as it is the part of the brain responsible for survival. As the bear approaches me, my limbic system retrieves survival information from a very distant and underperforming Boy Scout past. Which includes staying very still, waiting patiently until... POW! I punch the bear in the nose and watch in triumphant glory as it runs away in shame. Actually, that's the correct response for a shark—the bear tears me apart, limb from limb—but you can appreciate the elegant design and effort made by my limbic system to try and keep me alive.

The part of the brain that encourages a human to perform or repeat an action that promotes survival is called the "survival/reinforcement circuit." Its function is to reinforce an activity promoting survival, such as eating, drinking, or procreating.

This is also the part of the brain most affected by chemicals.

The survival/reinforcement circuit acts as a "Go" circuit. At the heart of this circuit is a part of the brain called the nucleus accumbens septi (NAc). In an effort to better understand the NAc, in the late 1950s, scientists conducted an experiment in which they rigged an electrode to a rat's NAc, which could be activated by a lever in its cage. The rat pressed the lever, received a little jolt to its NAc, then proceeded to press the lever five thousand times an hour until it died. The experiment's outcome wasn't affected when other survival stimuli like water, food, or rat company were placed in the cage. A different scientist conducted the same experiment, but with humans in the 1960s. The participants reported that the sensation was pleasurable; perhaps not oddly, they were drawn to pushing the lever over and over; in a mild but obsessively fueled manner.

The NAc, or Go circuit, tells us three things:

1. What you're doing is necessary for survival.
2. You should remember what you did for survival—escape, find food, gain comfort, relieve pain.
3. Do more of what you did until you are satisfied! (The constant message reinforces the importance of the action.)

Imagine I am in Egypt now, and I have decided to go for a walk in the desert. Being the scrupulous Boy Scout that I am, I do not tell anyone where I am going, and I don't bring any supplies. In other words, I am entirely unprepared for this little trek into the wilderness. Approximately twenty minutes later, I'm crawling on the sand, clothes reduced to rags and dying of thirst. My limbic system is driving me, overriding all thought and desire other than relieving my thirst. Then, through the haze of the heat, I see something incredible—a Diet Coke machine. I make it over the next dune and discover that the machine is, indeed, not a fragment of my imagination. I happen to have exact change and quickly buy a can of soda.[16]

As I take a swig, the deep craving, my thirst is finally quenched. "Ahhh!" I exclaim, just like in the commercials. Since the ego, especially mine, is incapable of ensuring the continued existence of our species by itself, survival memory remembers: "The next time I go for a walk, in the desert or otherwise, how about I don't forget something to drink?" Now, historically, I have found my response to anything pleasurable usually goes something like this: If one feels good, more must feel *awesome*. Even drinking too much water can kill a person, so to prevent me from drowning myself in Diet Coke, the brain has the means to turn off the Go circuit.

Interestingly, the part of the brain that predominantly shuts down the Go circuit resides in the neocortex, or the "thinking" brain, as opposed to the "reactive" survival brain, or limbic system. About 200,000 years ago, in Africa, our ancestors' frontal cortices folded onto themselves to accommodate the expansion of billions of new brain cells called neurons. This cognitive revolution is the anatomical origin of the modern human brain. And it is estimated we have 86

---

[16] A friend of mine read this and asked, "What exactly is the Diet Coke machine plugged into?" I still don't have an answer, so I didn't write him back.

billion neurons. Our sophisticated neocortex is associated with self-awareness, insight, decision-making, abstract thought, and it is tasked with regulating the impulses of the limbic system—which, remember, originated 250-300 million years ago. Sigmund Freud described this concept in his psychoanalytic theory when he wrote about the "super-ego" reigning in the primal urges of the "id."

Now, I assure you that when it comes to managing impulses before I entered recovery, delayed gratification—impulse control—was not a prominent part of my vocabulary, thinking, or life. However, I also assure you, my dedicated and patient reader, it is a *thing*.

Following a large release of dopamine, the part of the brain that shuts down the Go circuit is called the left orbitofrontal cortex, along with the fasciculus retroflexus and lateral habenula. Since there isn't a clever nickname or acronym for these parts of the brain, we'll refer to it as the "Stop" circuit. The Stop circuit releases glutamate (a neurotransmitter), which travels back to the ventral tegmental area and signals the cells to stop releasing dopamine, the neurotransmitter of the Go circuit. Glutamate also shuts down dopamine in the NAc.

To recap:

- Many people, past and present, have used chemicals to cope with their environment and enhance their existence.
- Powerful, refined mood-altering chemicals appeared in the past couple of hundred years, but the evolutionary timeline for Homo sapiens extends back hundreds of thousands of years.
- We have a survival brain or limbic system that unconsciously directs us toward activities conducive to our survival.
- This is the part of the brain **most** affected by chemicals, and it is **4-5x stronger** than the part of the brain responsible for making logical decisions and mitigating pleasure responses.
- Depending on how vital the survival need is, the limbic system can amplify the drive toward alleviating the craving.
- When a craving is satisfied, the Stop circuit shuts down the Go circuit by releasing glutamate—creating a feeling of satiation.
- Pleasure and survival overlap in the brain.

- Mood-altering chemicals bring about dopaminergic responses **100–1100%** more potent than other naturally occurring responses like sex, exercise, and food.

Crossing the Invisible Line

Chemicals affect the limbic system of everyone who consumes them. However, in certain people, the Go circuit will progressively override the Stop circuit, resulting in the "phenomenon of craving"—the drive to continue using chemicals despite consequences (i.e., *compulsion*). Additionally, there's permanent damage to the fasciculus retroflexus, which normally communicates a "stop" message to the Go circuit. Some people cross this invisible line after several uses. For others, it can be decades before they cross over from chemical use, misuse, or abuse into a full-fledged addiction. There are interesting variables and reasons that account for these differences, but they are for another time and another discussion. The critical thing to understand is that how addiction manifest is not uniform.[17]

What is also extremely important to understand is that this change in brain structure—the breakdown in communication between the Stop circuit and the NAc—is *permanent*. Additionally, the more a person uses chemicals, the stronger and more compromising the drive (craving) to use chemicals becomes. The compulsion to use can become so devastating that it supersedes even basic survival needs like food, safety, and sleep; it can grow in strength to the point where it overrides the need to care for your children.

Fortunately, the brain is an amazingly regenerative organ, and neural plasticity[18] can reprogram the limbic system and neocortex from "addicted" to "recovery" functioning. Though the breakdown in communication between the NAc (Go) and left orbitofrontal cortex (Stop) is permanent, and coincidentally, demonstrates how addiction meets criteria for the medical model of disease:

---

[17] The classic Twelve-Step suggestion to "look for the similarities as opposed to the differences" captures this sentiment perfectly.

[18] The brain's ability to change throughout the course of a lifetime. Well, at least until sixty years of age, based on current evidence.

Organ	Brain
Defect	The breakdown in communication between the NAc and left orbitofrontal cortex
Symptoms	Chemical use despite consequences; the loss of control; tolerance and withdrawal; cravings

Dr. Silkworth hypothesized alcoholics would have to abstain from alcohol permanently, lest the allergy reactivates the cycle of addiction. Personally, when I hear the word "allergy," my seasonal allergies and the accompanying symptoms come to mind. Silkworth was referring to the second definition of allergy: *an abnormal physical response.* And an abnormal physical response is what we just explored—the limbic system, pleasure/survival messages, dopamine and crossing the invisible line! Once someone develops an abnormal response to a specific chemical, they will almost always respond in this manner, irrespective of the length of time between uses.[19]

In the 1960s, scientists conducted experiments in which they gave rats unlimited access to cocaine via a lever they could press in their cage. Even with survival stimuli—water, food, company—in the cage, and a break from self-stimulation, the rats feverishly pressed the lever, consuming cocaine until they died. I understand that you, my lovely reader, are human, but rats respond to chemicals in the same order of preference as humans. Rats, unlike humans, do not have a moral compass, so the scientists concluded that addiction occurs because

YES
1. of the way the brain is designed
2. chemicals can subvert natural survival mechanisms

NO
1. morally corrupt rats making poor life decisions

Sociological, pharmacological, and other differences exist between chemicals and are a legitimate consideration to a certain extent. For

---

[19] Days, weeks, years, decades—*the rest of your life.*

example, there's a difference between having a glass of wine and taking several pulls from a crack pipe. But for all intents and purposes, to say "drugs and alcohol" is to make a distinction without a difference. Ethyl alcohol is an incredibly powerful central nervous system depressant, a drug that's arguably more detrimental than stimulants, other depressants, and hallucinogens combined. Alcohol's mortality rate in the United States is consistently second only to that of tobacco. All chemicals affect the limbic system, at either the ventral tegmental area, the hippocampus, or the NAc directly. All the same, the NAc will activate, and dopaminergic systems will fire up the Go circuit. The lack of distinction—concerning biological impact on the brain—the prevailing stigma of addiction, and ultimately arbitrary differences in mood-altering substances lead me to believe that the word "chemicals" is a more accurate and inclusive descriptor than "drugs and alcohol."

I learned this lesson the hard way because I would not accept the fact that I respond abnormally to chemicals due to a change in brain structure—or a breakdown in communication—beyond my own conscious volition. At one point or another, during nine years of active addiction, I was compromised by 3,4-Methylenedioxymethamphetamine, amphetamine salts and dextroamphetamine, marijuana, oxycodone, alcohol, heroin, cocaine, benzodiazepines, methadone, and, of course, nicotine. I am an extreme example of the disease of addiction. Not all addictions, though, are created equal. Some people have genetic predispositions that make them vulnerable to certain kinds of addictions (i.e., illnesses) while others have predispositions that protect against it.

By any objective measure, it is fair to say that I have abused benzodiazepines, such as Xanax and Valium, and I haven't ever *not* finished a bag of cocaine once I started using. But have I ever been as hopelessly and physiologically compromised by my benzodiazepine and cocaine use as I was by my amphetamine, alcohol, and opiate addictions?

No.

Does my somewhat manageable use of benzos and cocaine erase the reality of my hardcore addictions to amphetamines, alcohol, and opiates?

Of course not!

Suppose you have developed an addiction to your chemical of choice and are currently wondering whether you can successfully use another chemical that you have never abused (or even tried). In this case, the answer is *maybe at first*. Nevertheless, the propensity to develop an abnormal response to the chemical is nearly guaranteed given enough time and use of that chemical, or it will lead back to the substance(s) you were attempting to abstain from in the first place.

Unnecessary suffering, more addiction, or being elected to the cross-addiction hall of fame[20] are not prerequisites for surrendering to this truth:

Once you develop an abnormal response to a chemical, you will always respond that way—compulsively.

---

[20] Of which I am a ranking member.

THE OBSESSION OF THE MIND

"They are restless, irritable and discontented unless they can again experience the sense of ease and comfort which comes at once by taking a few drinks—drinks which they see others taking with impunity. After they have succumbed to the desire again, as so many do, and the phenomenon of craving develops... unless this person can experience an entire psychic change there is very little hope of his recovery."

—Dr. Silkworth

To comprehend *the obsession of the mind*, we must first understand how a memory is formed in the brain. Most memories last a lifetime because they are solid bits of protein imprinted on the brain as microscopic memory bumps called "dendritic spines." These tiny memory bumps grow on the dendrites of nerve cells when the nerves are stimulated by sensory input. Emotionally charged memories, such as the birth of a first child, are more deeply imprinted than everyday memories, like changing the cat litter. These emotionally salient experiences result in the creation of more dendritic spines.

When our ancestors began cultivating and selling land, they would finalize a deal by holding their hands over a candle, both literally and figuratively burning the memory of the transaction into their shared consciousness. In medieval times, a king would order his young prince thrown into a cold body of water to emotionally-charge, or more deeply imprint, the memory of his aunt's wedding, which he had been less than thrilled to attend in the first place (imagine that).

When I say, "emotionally charged memories," I mean memories created from a large chemical release between neurons.[21] Little bits of protein called "peptides" constitute our emotions or feelings. Some neuropeptides (i.e., occurring in the brain) correlate with pleasure and intoxication. Intoxicants mirror the shape of these molecules and thus induce a euphoric response in the mind and body when ingested.

Remember:

- Chemicals (uppers, downers, and all arounders) affect the pleasure/survival part of the brain **100–1100%** more powerfully and reliably than average sensory input like food, sex, and exercise.
- The stronger the chemical, the more rapid it grows and proliferates memory bumps on the dendrites—the more deeply imprinted the memory becomes.
- Whatever you learn and remember governs future behavior.
- The more we repeat a behavior, the more likely we are to repeat that behavior when faced with a similar situation
- There's no guarantee you will make the "best" decision using executive function—that is, the neocortex.
- Instinct defers to whatever feels most comfortable, is quickest, easiest, or works the greatest, and it resides in the more powerful limbic system.

What does this mean for addiction? First, the brain wrongly interprets our chemical use as conducive to survival because pleasure and survival overlap in the brain. Second, the chemical use experience deeply imprints on the brain's emotional memory system.[22] The memory is labeled as the greatest amount of "relief" or "security" concerning personal needs met during the time of intoxication.[23] And for those who have yet to try—let me tell you—extinguishing an

---

[21] The formal jargon is *action potential*.

[22] Known as the *amygdala* and *hippocampus*. The amygdala relates to conditioned response ("people, places, and things"), the hippocampus euphoric recall.

[23] In other words, *reward-related associations*.

addicted limbic system's preference for chemicals is no easy feat! For example, one way to alleviate loneliness is to explore a community, connect with other people, serve a purpose outside oneself. Another way is to use chemicals to numb the pain and emptiness of being alone without having to leave the couch. Although the former is less destructive, and, admittedly, a healthier approach to making friends, the latter more deeply imprints the survival brain because the chemical use charges the experience. After months or years of chemical-use behavior, these responses become automatic or instinctual at a survival level. Thus, in early recovery and faced with the prospect of leaving the environment that's most comfortable and strongly associated with chemicals, it will take a concerted effort to work through the dissonance and pull of the survival brain's preference to do what's most familiar—use chemicals and veg out.

Because memories last a lifetime, chemical abuse creates what I call "the seed of relapse." These robust dopamine-related imprints are located in the amygdalae and hippocampal areas of the brain.[24] While recovery can arrest cravings for chemicals and related behaviors, memories of euphoric experiences never disappear; they merely become dormant.[25] To illustrate how deeply these memories imprint themselves, I'll share from personal experience. Even after a decade of being in recovery, if I recall emotional memory information from my amygdala and hippocampus related to my chemical use, I can vividly recall the smell of cheap vodka,[26] the taste of an amphetamine or cocaine drip after insufflation, the bitter taste of psilocybin mushrooms eaten raw, the taste of brown heroin, the burn and smell of a cigarette after a large meal... I could go on, but doing so serves no purpose other than reinforcing this biological truth: Pleasure and intoxication from chemical use more deeply imprint the brain relative to the pain and suffering of using those same chemicals. And that's not to say emotionally charged experiences that are painful or otherwise negative don't also deeply imprint on the brain—they do.

My disease came to a final cusp when my liver found itself unable to continue metabolizing the liquor and heroin I was consuming. The

---

[24] But with a bias to the right hemisphere.

[25] Formally called *neurotraces*.

[26] The amygdala is intimately connected to the olfactory system. Take a minute to think of all your wonderful smell-oriented memories.

alcohol my liver couldn't filter kept circulating in my bloodstream. Blood poisoning took over, and I approached death itself. In hindsight, I genuinely believe I should have died the night before finally being admitted to a hospital. The doctors I encountered at Northwestern Memorial Hospital in downtown Chicago the following morning (during a self-imposed 72-hour psychiatric hold) had no scientific explanation of why I was still alive when I arrived.[27] It is a horrendous experience when your alcoholism kills you with blood poisoning. Your blood is boiling with migraine intensity; death is violently attempting to exit the body. It's all happening painfully slowly—every moment becoming increasingly sick and out of control. Delirious. Executive function all but dissipates. In and out of consciousness the spirit—the will to live—barely clings to its destroyed vessel. Sounds awful, I know. But compared to the most potent experiences I've had with intoxication, I recall this near-death experience, for the most part, only intellectually. This lapse in physical memory may explain why so many individuals in early recovery believe that a short-term consequence, or an accumulation of negative experiences, will alone motivate and ensure long-term success. Let us not forget; all feelings are *fleeting*, including good ones, like the resolve and motivation to abstain from chemicals.

The person in early recovery is still programmed for chemical use. This is because the brain defers to what is familiar and easy. After years of daily chemical use and multiple extended periods of around-the-clock use, the chemicals became deeply intertwined with every aspect of my life. Waking up in the morning and recalling my own existence was enough to trigger the desire to use chemicals. Hence, as I began living a life in sobriety, the disease sneakily directed my thoughts back to chemicals anytime I was stressed, uncomfortable, lonely, bored, depressed, angry, fearful—feelings influential in fueling my chemical use in active addiction. Not only did I have to train my mind, body, and spirit to live another way, I had to do so while working through the mountain of problems accumulated during a decade of untreated addiction and nearly two decades of mostly

---

[27] Retrograde extrapolation-based math (see the last page) shows my approximate blood alcohol content (BAC) at the time of passing out was 0.687. A BAC of 0.4 and above is associated with coma and death from respiratory arrest.

undiagnosed mental illness. Making matters most challenging[28] was my limbic system incessantly badgering my commitment and need for recovery. As if early recovery isn't hard enough!

When we consider the abundance of challenges in early recovery, it begins to make sense why outside support is so paramount when treating addiction. Addiction is not about being weak, morally corrupt, intrinsically bad, or any silliness like that. It's about the limbic system overriding the neocortex, intoxication imprinting itself deeply into emotional memory, and remaining programmed for chemical use despite sobering up.

One afternoon, a despairing, newly sober man reached out to me after a lecture. He painfully recounted his recent struggles working with others in his residential unit. Exasperated, he rhetorically jeered, "If my rugged individualism and solitary approach to solving problems hasn't let me down yet, why should I make an effort to care about others?"[29] I asked him what he did for a living. He told me he was a construction manager. I asked him if he constructed buildings by himself or if he used a crew. With a crew, he confirmed. I told him no matter the extent of his intelligence and ability, he would not take on a job as important as his *alone*. No. He would use a team to achieve something greater than his individual effort alone. He looked me in the eye with an expression of surprising clarity, thanked me, and hurried back to his unit.

Dopamine is a neurotransmitter of survival and pleasure, but it is also one of anticipation. Remember Pavlov's dogs—through operant conditioning, the dogs came to associate the ringing of a bell with being fed. But did you know that the dogs began to salivate when Pavlov first entered the room? Scientists have conducted experiments with mice and chimpanzees[30] wherein a light illuminates before the delivering of a stimulus (a treat) that produces a dopamine response. After sufficient conditioning, seeing only the light flash will bring about the anticipatory dopamine response.

Have you ever been in withdrawal from opiates? Finally, after receiving a call from your dealer to come get the chemicals, you find yourself slightly less compromised by your withdrawal symptoms—

---

[28] And ironic if we're not taking me too seriously–*and we aren't*.

[29] I might be superimposing counselor language onto what he actually said.

[30] Genetically, our closest relatives.

even possibly intoxicated or giddy in a mild-mannered way. Weird huh? Alternatively, maybe one evening, you find yourself irritable, restless, and somewhat discontent to be dragged to a neighborhood function by your significant other. But after arriving, you learn there's alcohol available. And not only that, other like-minded people with whom to drink it! All of a sudden, your attitude and spirit for the evening have mysteriously changed for the better. Personally, what I craved even more than the intoxication from chemicals was the idea and the pursuit of intoxication. In other words, a perfectly satiated, enduring experience climbing "dopamine mountain."

Life is Stressful

Recent science tells us that the obsession to use chemicals is occurring predominantly below the level of conscious awareness. In recovery, this is concerning as we are consistently sober and operating at a conscious level (at least I hope we are). The dissonance of a limbic system trained to relieve stress with chemicals and a neocortex committed to sobriety can feed the desire to use chemicals. A person can have all the reasons in the world to stay sober, but a subtle, growing urge to use a chemical persists. At times, the euphoric recall—the stress-relieving memories—are so vivid you can almost taste them. Then guilt and shame reemerge, as a recollection of all the consequences from using chemicals comes back to haunt you.

Furthermore, because stress is a constant in life, you must approach the problems, successes, and in-betweens of your life in a manner that does not trigger the euphoric imprints.[31] If we do not arrest the illness, these addiction-related networks remain activated, festering, and growing in strength. Unresolved, the obsession of the mind eventually convinces logic, "I won't lose control again..." "It'll be different this time..." Even though maybe, somewhere deep in the pit of your stomach, you know that's not true. In a spiritual approach to life, such as the Twelve Steps, a superficial practice almost always results in an

---

[31] In an addicted individual, stress directly correlates with the craving response for chemical use. Therefore, a "spiritual" solution, such as equanimity and inner peace—not fleeting intoxication/pleasure from chemical use—is the logical and sustainable solution to the reality of stress.

unmanaged stress response. Either a person accesses a source of strength within and without themselves and works through their problems, or they do not. If they don't, the likelihood of returning to the people, places, and things (but especially chemicals) before attempting recovery is not an *if* but rather a *when*.

In early recovery, when a person experiences stress, the brain's smoke detector, the amygdala, sounds off, which leads to activation of the NAc by way of the thalamus, hippocampus, and prefrontal cortex resulting in a craving for "relief."[32] One who has been using chemicals more often than not in response to the challenges (stressors) in their life can expect a craving at an unconscious level for chemical-related relief. Unfortunately, not only have our survival mechanisms been subverted—causing the phenomenon of craving and the irrational nature of the disease itself—but intoxication is imprinted as "pro-survival" in emotional memory.

People in early recovery must begin to dispel the notion they are not experiencing cravings. Yes, they might not be registering at the level of conscious awareness, but they are occurring! Imagine the recovery stress/craving correlation as an addicted car engine. Operating a vehicle requires fuel, in our case chemicals. Driving the car taxes it. Stress accumulates in the form of wear and tear on the motor. What's helpful to remember is that our central nervous system is like a motor. And the resilience of this motor becomes worn down as a direct result of our chemical use and related stressors. Consequently, a newly sober but worn-down motor will experience cravings when running at capacity for an extended time—or, acutely, for no reason at all. What this means in human terms is that you must conscientiously and diligently manage your stress load and cravings in order to arrest the illness.

Stress is a certainty of life. Though, in early sobriety, we find our overall tolerance for stress is quite low. We find ourselves becoming irritable, frustrated, restless, impatient, and sometimes completely flustered.[33] It's not too long before the cumulative stress response triggers the seed of relapse. A message makes its way from the limbic

---

[32] In this analogy, the release of stress hormones is the "alarm." The smoke detector-amygdala analogy I borrowed from Dr. Bessel van der Kolk's seminal work, *The Body Keeps the Score.*

[33] Stress sensitivity à la post-acute withdrawal syndrome.

system to the neocortex, where the nonverbal impulse translates to "Using a chemical would feel good right about now. Wouldn't it?"

Thus, an unfortunate paradox:

Using chemicals for stress relief, emotional regulation, escape, social connection or pleasure in the short-term is ultimately overwhelmed by the abundance of neglected stress, problems, cravings, and consequences in the long run.

This conundrum can explain why previous moments of clarity and attempts at sobriety have been unfruitful: You find yourself backed into a corner of stress and ineptitude. And despite a serious, even desperate, effort to do the right thing, to change for the better, there's a lack of internal resources, strength, or "Power" to free ourselves from our suffering. Like Dr. Silkworth said, "...restless, irritable, and discontented." Defeated, we return to using chemicals well aware of the reality we will eventually lose control, but helpless... because there are no other means to alleviate the pain and eradicate the craving. I oddly found some level of comfort in the way in which my chemical use hurt me—its inevitability—at least I knew what to expect.

Remember how chemicals have an affinity for survival mechanisms in the brain? Well, this region of the brain is also intimately connected to the autonomic nervous system. Intoxication, acute or long-term, activates the sympathetic nervous system.[34] This hyper-aroused state[35] is such that the physiological reactions create additional stress that becomes chronic in active addiction. In other words, the "stress switch" stays in the *on* position. As a result, systems become taxed, leading to a wide-awake form of exhaustion, a run-down immune system, greater vulnerability to illness, and you bet—more stress.

Let's return to the car engine analogy of our motor being exhausted from the use of chemicals. Your nervous system is the motor in recovery from addiction. Stress taxes the motor. If stress is not effectively processed; it accumulates in the body. Challenges, such as strained relationships, financial and economic insecurity, euphoric

---

[34] The "excitatory nervous system," as opposed to the parasympathetic nervous system, or "calm–digestive–vegetative nervous system."
[35] Increased heart rate and blood pressure, constricted blood vessels, dilated pupils, inhibited digestion.

recall, mental illness, boredom, resentment, guilt and shame are familiar and precipitate relapse. In fact, because of a worn-down motor from the stress switch being left on, managing *any* stress will be difficult. Since chemical use has become the fuel powering your motor—as it does to some degree in everyone compromised by addiction—chemical-sourced relief will remain the preference in early recovery. Therefore, more than a strong commitment to sobriety is needed. A community can literally buffer the stress response as well as support change and growth. Admittedly, it is a serious undertaking to overhaul a motor. But this much is true: Recovery behaviors and social support can facilitate neuroadaptations that arrest a substance use disorder, bringing about "remission" and freedom from cravings.

To achieve this, recovery must consist of two parts:

1. Accessing new sources of fuel to run the motor
2. Sustaining a connection to those sources

When challenged by stress in early recovery, prepare for the reality, there will be times when your motor screams for (craves) old fuel. A newly sober but addicted motor will seek out the people, places, and things associated with chemicals. This attraction stems from the imprinting of intoxication on emotional memory systems.[36] These euphoric imprints fuel a challenging aspect of early recovery—being preprogrammed for potent chemical-mediated relief while learning new strategies for managing stress. And because there are countless hiccups in recovery ("life"), it probably is not a surprise to learn that between 40 and 60 percent of people relapse in their first year of recovery from addiction.[37] I do not share these statistics to add to the difficult feelings you may currently be experiencing; rather, I share them to highlight the challenging and taxing nature of early recovery.

In a spiritual approach to recovery, a person does not have the luxury of passivity or relying on loved ones to deter chemical use, or pretending the problem isn't as serious as it is. We must gain access to a source of strength and resilience—a new fuel source—within and without ourselves. Otherwise, the stress response cumulatively grows.

---

[36] In other words, the *seed of relapse*© planted in the hippocampus and amygdala.
[37] In the field long-term recovery is typically understood to be five years. How humbling! Everything up until five years is "early recovery."

It fuels addicted-related networks and thus the craving to seek relief from using chemicals.

This biological reality is why I remain in recovery to this very day. I have recovered from a hopeless state of mind and body, but the disease of addiction remains planted in my survival memory for the remainder of my life. And because the part of my brain that regulates my response to mood-altering chemicals will never change in favor of a controlled response to intoxication, *not* using chemicals is the only option.

I face the truth:

Either grow spiritually or die from my disease.

THE MALADY OF THE SPIRIT

"As long as pleasure is our end, we will be dishonest with ourselves and with those we love. We will not seek their good but only our own pleasure. Authentic love requires times of self-sacrifice. It requires that people monitor the sensations and feelings and mood of others, not just those of themselves."

—Thomas Merton

The spiritual solution to addiction is not well understood. Upon first consideration, it is seen as antiscientific fluff. Nevertheless, the evidence is this: Tens of millions of people have found sustained relief from the obsession of the mind, as well as the boredom and emptiness of sobriety. Compulsion-fueled selfishness is transformed into love and service. And not only are afflicted persons healed in body and mind, but how they experience the world, and the sources of Power from which they draw, have inexplicably changed them for the better.

Irrespective of belief systems or faith traditions, these people are simultaneously drawing from a source of strength seemingly infinite in its supply.[38] Of course, the continued access to this strength is contingent upon the effort to grow in a spiritual approach to life.

If I were to ask a group of theologians to define the word "religion," I am guessing they would be hard-pressed to agree on a standard definition. A definition that I believe captures this behemoth of a subject: *a set of dogma explaining man's existence*. Asking life's biggest questions and seeking the answers in our lives is essential (at least I hope so). Doing so is not required to treat addiction, recover from a hopeless state of mind and body consequent of addiction, or

---

[38] In my humble opinion.

sustain long-term recovery from addiction. Religion may provide answers to how we got here or how to approach and find meaning in life, but it is not required when approaching a spiritual walk in life.

The spiritual solution is frequently criticized as a treatment for the disease of addiction. The person with insulin-dependent Type 1 diabetes isn't asked to turn their will and life over to the care of a Higher Power or attend meetings or be of service to other diabetics. How is can this be a solution for addiction? Well, considering the extensive challenges associated with diabetes, including high relapse rates, comorbid physical and mental illness, and premature death, one could ask why society isn't looking at more comprehensive solutions for managing diabetes beyond nutritional training and medication management. The delivery of quality treatment to the person with diabetes doesn't appear to be the problem. Instead, the diabetic's willingness, or *spirit*, to manage their chronic illness is. Thus, a spiritual component is necessary when it comes to treating a chronic illness.

What is spirituality? For some, this means a personal relationship with a Higher Power, or God, of their own understanding. Where they're inclined to seek their Higher Power's will in lieu of their own. If this approach to spirituality does not work for you, now or ever, that's completely all right! I present the following definitions of spirituality for your consideration, with the caveat they are interdependent and addressed with honest effort and seriousness:

1. How we find meaning in our life
2. Our relationship to what is most important to us
3. Interconnectedness

Active addiction is the most brutal and tiresome prison in which I have ever resided. A compulsion beyond my physical and mental control but also relentlessly habitual. Using chemicals became an integral part of living my life. I could not manage the relationship with my person without them. Sitting at a desk or plastered on some cheap futon, for hours upon hours, I consumed chemicals:

- To escape
- To create a foundation of normalcy
- To numb feelings
- To feel good
- To hurt
- To fall asleep
- To fill the voids
- To celebrate
- To relate meaningfully with other people
- To love
- To tolerate my very existence

In the end, the disease reduced my life to a one-block radius. There was a liquor store across the street, and my dealer delivered. I quit eating. My liver began losing the final battle of the war metabolizing the poisons I had subjected it to on a near-daily basis for eight years. As I mentioned earlier, I survived long enough to admit myself to a three-day psychiatric hospitalization at Northwestern hospital. But I could not stop drinking. When the craving for alcohol returned, I made a ruckus and prepared to leave. Two doctors told me I would be dead by the end of the week. I left anyway. Prescribed Valium for withdrawal, I returned to drinking and taking the benzo with it. Two days later, I went to my doctor and played him for a prescription of Librium and some other downer I cannot remember.[39] I'm unsure if it was reverse tolerance or the synergism[40] between the alcohol and benzos, or some combination of both. But instead of the 1-1.5 liters of vodka, I typically consumed every twenty-four hours, it now only took 375 mL (pint) to become intoxicated—but not in a pleasant manner.

No, in a way that was killing me.

I drank and used chemicals to the point of death itself.

Most likely, your plight with chemicals has not taken you that far. Unimaginable pain and suffering are not a prerequisite for recovery. But I am curious if your chemical use has caused you hopelessness, if addiction has left you powerlessness and paralyzed with fear and

---

[39] Dr. Wesley Cook, I am sorry I manipulated you for those scripts, but the medications ultimately served their purpose (safely detoxing myself from alcohol), and the flyer you gave me got me to an A.A. meeting that saved my life.

[40] Metabolization of multiple central nervous depressants in the liver results in a more powerful intoxicated state.

desperation and deteriorated your purpose in life. Admittedly, addiction will get you out of bed in the morning, especially if you are as enthusiastic about alleviating withdrawal as I am when dependent on amphetamines, opioids, and/or alcohol. But have you ever woken up one morning, deep in the throes of your addiction, and in a moment of honest self-reflection asked yourself, "What's the point?" Seriously, is the despair in your life growing at an alarming pace? Is there a blaring deficit, an emptiness, an unquenchable hole emerging or reemerging in your being and life? A void that even an endless flow of chemicals can't manage. Why continue pursuing goals and life itself if it is a foregone conclusion that the majority of your time and energy will be consumed and ruined by your chemical use? Why even get out of bed? What's the point to any of this?

That, my friend, is a *broken* spirit.

When I was in early recovery, the hopelessness and fear, the post-acute withdrawal and mental illness were nearly unbearable. But my sober community provided new meaning and hope. They were the strength I needed to persevere. They taught me about my illness, provided unconditional positive regard despite my sick, despairing, and intimidating presentation. They suggested I look for the things that connect me with my fellow brother or sister instead of the things that separate us. My community suggested I be of service to others suffering from addiction and that being of service meant loving and expecting nothing in return. They held me accountable to my chronic, progressive, and prone-to-relapse disease; the reality that if my disease retook control, I would die.

As I began taking care of myself seriously, for the first time in a long time—arguably ever—I found a new purpose. Surprisingly, it was inside of *me*. I came to understand the divine paradox: helping others unconditionally brings about an experience with the highest value in all of the human experience: *agape*. And what purpose it is! It is such a beautiful thing; no matter how down, hopeless, and lonely it gets, I can always be useful to my fellow human in recovery. I understand if the notion of helping others while also facing the breadth of your situation sounds unappealing, or even ludicrous. But doesn't it make sense, on some level, that helping others is a viable solution to addiction? Particularly when we consider how selfish, self-centered and self-seeking the illness actually is?

In active addiction, my demands are endless. I give marginally, at best, and expect *everything* in return. I have never been emptier, more alone, and lacking in meaning in my life.[41]

I challenge you, my fearless reader, to deny that your chemical use hasn't wrought a comparable void in your own life. In recovery, or what I understand to be a spiritual walk in life, I give endlessly and expect nothing in return. By the divine paradox, I access a sustainable reward—a source of strength, equanimity, and joy—that enables me to walk through strife, uncertainty, fear, and even tragedy with a new sense of purpose. Taking spiritual growth seriously enables me to face success with a new capacity for humility. I'm never alone because the love I give my fellow human grows a love inside of me. There's a presence, a strength, an *aliveness* intertwined with the fabric of my being. A Power that wasn't there before I began walking a spiritual path. I am at peace with myself. My autonomy and freedom are greater than ever before. How miraculous—through spiritual change, community support, service to others, and neuroadaptations of the highest order, we can be saved from addicted suffering and premature death.

In Need of "Real" Power

Step Twelve mentions a spiritual awakening "as a result of these Steps," which means that my spirit, or the will to face my own life, has awoken in a manner clearly absent before working the Steps. And that describes my experience, which is amazingly typical when honestly approaching Twelve-Step recovery. I continue to draw from this source of Power to this very day, and I believe—based on over a decade of faith-based experiences—that this source of strength and spiritual fuel is infinite. I haven't received answers to the mysteries of the universe, but neither has anyone else. And I don't believe that's the point. The point is that there is Power beyond chemicals, materialism, striving, accomplishment, and social influence—sources of personal strength from which I have tried to draw, but always ending in dissatisfaction and emptiness. I'm at peace with myself and

---

[41] If you identify as a super responsible person, think of how poorly you have been taking care of yourself relative to those you care for.

the world. However, I can never stop seeking this Power in my life. The plot never deviates from the all-too-familiar relapse story: A person stops managing their chronic disease, stress accumulates, the seed of relapse activates, cravings reemerge, and relapse occurs irrespective of whether they believe the response to chemicals will be different or not. But I have met those, too, who have walked a spiritual path throughout most of their life, and they have something I want.

Something tangible but spiritual in nature.

In Viktor Frankl's classic book *Man's Search for Meaning*, the German psychiatrist finds himself called out—by a close friend, no less—and subsequently imprisoned by the Nazis in 1942. Surviving four different concentration camps, he would later learn his entire family had been killed.[42] Frankl described two kinds of prisoners: the first, unable to envision a future, died; the second, appeared to draw strength from serving a purpose outside themselves—like a spouse, their fellow prisoners, or God. This intention became a reprieve from their suffering. It fueled the will to endure despite indescribably cruel and horrific circumstances. By facing fear and hopelessness head-on and working through it with some sense of purpose, Frankl survived this waking nightmare until Allied Forces freed him in 1945.

In his words:

> *We must never forget that we may also find meaning in life even when confronted with a hopeless situation, when facing a fate that cannot be changed. For what then matters is to bear witness to the uniquely human potential at its best, which is to transform a personal tragedy into a triumph, to turn one's predicament into a human achievement. When we are no longer able to change a situation—just think of an incurable disease such as inoperable cancer—we are challenged to change ourselves.*

From a world history perspective, Power is the primary pursuit of humans. Power is synonymous with the pursuit of *more*. In that case, do not be shocked to learn the desire for Power predominantly resides

---

[42] Except a single sister.

in the limbic system. That's right; the conscious desire for more fuels the stronger and more relentless survival brain to crave and seek it out.

But is the pursuit of more—wealth, security, and influence—worth my time and effort?

Well, since the pleasure center is affected by these pursuits in a similar way to how a chemical affects the limbic system, I can predict they'll never provide the relief or Power I need. The drugs and alcohol were 11x stronger!

Can we earnestly proclaim ourselves superior to our animal brethren if the ultimate end in life is to obtain material wealth beyond our basic needs? Consumption for the sake of consumption?

Please understand me. I'm not knocking survival. I just think we have a deep need to be in communion with one another, to contribute to something that transcends our contribution, to treat others the way we would have them treat us. We must grow our spiritual condition to reconcile the void left by chemicals, to achieve "real" wholeness.

There was a time when I equated chemicals with philosophical and personal meaning. Erroneously, I used intoxication as my primary source of spiritual relief, resilience, even happiness itself. Basing these matters on something as fleeting as intoxication always ended with feeling disappointed, hopeless, and empty. Until I began basing my self-worth in a disciplined approach to life, I would never find any lasting meaning.

Don't forget. The pull to return to the spiritual hellhole of addiction can be up to four to five times stronger than your will not to. Without a new spiritual experience, one in which you find meaning, purpose, strength, and peace, your chances of recovery diminish greatly. It might sound outlandish, but if you seriously consider the degree of difficulty recovering from addiction, I believe you will also conclude a personal breakthrough, or "psychic change" as described by Dr. Silkworth, is necessary to bring about long-term recovery.

I once watched a documentary about a married couple living with insulin-dependent Type 1 diabetes. The man and his wife were morbidly obese and struggling with their eating habits. The producers orchestrated a snapshot of their life: binging on large buckets of fried chicken, junk food, sweets and candy; a liter of soda constituting one serving—and consuming, on average, three-a-day; their recliners moaning under the weight of their bodies as they watched television. Embarrassed, but with grins on their faces, they shrugged at the camera in a manner that said, "What can you do?" The show cut to the next scene and the man meets with his doctor to discuss his "out of control" diabetes. The doctor explains, sternly, there has been so much damage to his right foot (neuropathy) that if he doesn't make immediate lifestyle changes—improving his diet, exercising, and losing weight—the next time he sees him, they will have to amputate his foot.[43]

So, guess who loses his foot?

With respects to addiction, I can completely relate!

I cannot say with absolute certainty, but I can't imagine having a foot amputated for reasons stemming from poorly managed diabetes is a *positive* value. Ask someone whether they would prefer to hold onto their appendages or not, and I'm confident the response will be holding onto their body parts. Indeed, this is why we must discuss spiritual matters when managing a chronic, progressive, and prone-to-relapse illness. We cannot force an individual to manage their disease, but we can motivate them and provide accountability.

Recovery from addiction faces the same reality. But what if the addicted person does not want help? As a society, if we want improved outcomes with addiction and other chronic illnesses, a discussion about taking personal responsibility for the disease must occur.

It is easier to not take care of myself than it is to take care of myself. I cannot imagine I'm unique in that. But if taking care of myself is an important matter (and it is), then the energy I exert towards that intention will most reflect my ability to apply it in life.

[whispers]: Talking about change does not necessarily lead to change.

Action requires me to exert my will.[44] But I'm tired and a little lazy. And what an incredible time to be alive, human, and lazy! In our modern and ultra-sedentary American society, everything is tailor-made to modulate the pleasure center and fuel consumption. The standard American diet—red meat, refined sugar, saturated fat, and, typically, high sodium—isn't the healthiest. But it tastes amazing and feels so good! My middle name is "carbs." I eat the pizza, crash, crave more carbs, eat, ad infinitum. What can you do? The major suppliers of food in this country sell cheap processed products designed to make

---

[43] Chronically elevated blood sugar levels damages blood vessels and can lead to problems in the eyes, heart, and extremities.

[44] Desire is an abstraction, whereas exertion of one's will is desire *plus* action.

me irrationally purchase more of them. Then, to make the consumerism even more titillating, sexually suggestive content in advertisements are used to sell everything from hamburgers to car tires to bug spray. You, my discerning reader, probably understand why advertisers do this. Of course, you do—it's because bug spray is boring. But if we use sex to grab the attention of the limbic system, maybe our mind will drift in favor of purchasing whatever nonsense is flashing on the television screen.[45]

When it comes to taking care of myself, I have found it most effective to do so in a holistic manner—body, mind, and spirit. I can choose to focus on only one aspect of my health; although, it will ultimately be at the expense of total well-being.

- To take care of my **body**: I exercise two to three times per week; make regular visits to my physician, dentist, psychotherapist, and psychiatrist—and follow their recommendations (mostly); prioritize sleep hygiene; get deep tissue massages; balance caloric intake with what I burn; and moderate my input of diet soda (ahem, I try).

- To take care of my **mind**: I read daily; keep current with the news; ask deep questions; continue professional study and research; enjoy my hobbies; and ensure that my subjective frame of reference—my autobiographical experience in life—is grounded in reality and devoid of significant distortions.

- To take care of my **spirit**: I pray, meditate, and practice mindfulness every day; have a yoga practice; pursue goals that require personal growth; practice gratitude; do service work; avoid isolation, engage my fellow brothers and sisters and, critically, align my actions with my belief system.

I cannot thank my community enough for holding me accountable to this never-ending challenge. A long time ago, I made several meager attempts to address my addictions through superficial treatment effort and cynical Twelve-Step meeting attendance.

---

[45] Later, presumably in your pajamas, under the painful fluorescent lighting of some warehouse mega store.

However, until I was willing to be accountable and align my actions with my values, the chances of bringing about change in my life were slim to none.

What is most important to you?

- Being true to yourself

- Taking care of your family

- Having security and freedom in your life

- Pursuing goals and dreams

- Being creative

- Knowing inner peace

The part of the brain in which I feel safe and secure is my limbic system. Pursuing value and serving what's most important to me as a human resides in my frontal cortex. What happens if I do not push myself beyond the limbic system's preference for routine and predictability? Will I ever be deeply satisfied and at peace?

One evening, I was studying research about solitary confinement[46] and learned that there are good data showing severe isolation is harmful to *all* prisoners. And not only that, but solitary confinement is more detrimental to those with preexisting mental illness—that is, for more than half the entire prison population. Humans are herd creatures; we do not appear to fare too well when separated for extended periods from other humans. Even monks who take a vow of silence do so in communion with other monks. Our grandparents live longer when they have a pet or, even better, when they live with family. Recent studies have determined that the health risks associated with loneliness are greater than those of obesity, smoking, exercise, or nutrition. When we consider that members of our species share

---

[46] Wild weekend, I know.

between 99%–99.9% genetic material, we begin to see that not only do we need one another, but we have a whole lot in common.

Self-reliance will not suffice. It cannot work because it ignores the biological reality that humans thrive in settings with other humans, not when they are alone. I know it looks cool to be *that* badass, who seemingly doesn't need anyone—trail-blazing through life without consequences—but even the most rugged loner needs connection with their fellow human.

Addiction is an incredibly isolating illness. Basking in the glow of intoxication, I would ask myself: "Should I venture out into the unknown and put forth my most authentic and attractive person? Take a risk? Be vulnerable? Or should I stay in and use chemicals?"

At first, chemicals propelled me forward, leaps and bounds concerning personal confidence and social graces. Nonetheless, no matter what I did, the chemicals and isolation would eventually take over. My mother and a hostage (girlfriend) stayed around the longest, tumbling into my pit of addiction with me. But there came the point when neither of them could associate with me. They could no longer participate in the personal hell I had created, so they removed themselves from my life. I kept falling into that hole. Two hundred numbers in my phone, and I had burned every single bridge.

I thought I could be alone forever so long as my buzz, my escape, my chemicals didn't fail me.

But chemicals will always fail you.

It is a progressive illness. Eventually, you reach the point where no combination of chemicals will register a euphoric response.[47] Of course, you continue using. What else can you do? The body becomes taxed in its ability to process the poisons it is being subjected to on a daily, even hourly, basis. The desire for sustenance leaves you, and an even stronger desire to use chemicals takes precedence. Fear, which has been increasingly creeping into prominence, becomes all-encompassing. All that's left is a chemically addicted animal shackled to a prison of its own (partial) creation: life reduced to a one-block radius; pressing the lever five thousand times an hour; praying for death, because death now appears to be the only viable answer to the pain; and the pain is only getting worse.

---

[47] An abnormally high hedonic setpoint consequent of severely downregulated dopaminergic systems.

Before you freak out, remember, there are an estimated twenty-three to twenty-five million Americans in recovery from addiction right now. That said, I don't believe change and long-term recovery can occur in isolation. Problems are not created in a vacuum. Accordingly, the solution is not found in one either. A spiritual walk in life means relating to my fellow brothers and sisters in an authentic and meaningful way. It doesn't mean I'm going to be friends with everyone (I'm not) or like everyone (I don't), but it does mean I create and maintain a reliable support system. Relationships will come and go, people will die from addiction, new people will get sober, but the constant, for us as social recovering beings, must be connectedness with other human beings.

The biggest leap of faith I have ever taken was the trust I put in my recovery community in early recovery. It was terrifying and painfully uncomfortable to accept help from others when I was unable to control or trust myself. No matter what effort I put forth in active addiction, ultimately, it was inevitable, I would crumble under the weight of craving, intoxication, and isolation. Practically speaking, if you cannot trust your own behavior due to a compulsion beyond your physical and mental control, how are you supposed to trust anyone else?

What else can you do but trust? Is there any other option?

Martin Luther King, Jr. said, "Faith is taking the first step when you can't see the whole staircase." He is right of course. The most constructive action I could have taken in early recovery was reaching outside of myself for support, then overhauling my relationship with myself.[48] Webster's second definition of faith is: *to put trust in a person or thing.* So, in a way, addiction is one of the ultimate expressions of faith. My chemical use was my ultimate emotional reprieve. Chemicals fueled my entire existence. It was my solution to the problem of separateness from my fellow humans. It was my faith, and it was going to kill me. However, the principle was the same: I trusted in a Higher Power outside of myself and prayed that the chemicals would be my salvation.[49] That sounds silly when I say it aloud, but I'm in good company. Many have attempted a similar form

---

[48] Which, if I am being honest, was not the epitome of health and positivity before I began using chemicals at the ripe age of fifteen.

[49] There's an excellent chance you are not as sick as I once was.

of chemical-based faith in their approach to life. And so many, like me, have been let down.

How do we come to trust in anything?

What about a new relationship with a person?

People are tricky because you never know what sneaky, self-interested things they're up to or if you are unwittingly a pawn in some scheme of theirs. Maybe I'm just paranoid? Either way, my history consistently demonstrates that I do not make new friends very easily.

You suggest we should meet up for coffee to discuss that *thing* we are both crazy about. I hesitantly agree when you specify a time and place.

Will you cancel at the last moment?

Will you forget altogether and leave me there at the coffee shop looking like a dork, so naïve, trusting in the integrity of a fellow human being?

No. You show up.

We have an excellent conversation. Reveal an appropriate and more forthcoming amount of information about ourselves. We make plans to do that *thing* we both enjoy. Fear whispers silly little nothings in my ear. I show up, and so do you! We have a great time sharing our passion. Vulnerability increases and we grow closer to the other. Later on, unexpectedly, you reach out to me in a time of need. I show up because I care. When something happens in my own life, I call you. You are there for me. What was once empty space and uncertainty between us has become a bond based on reciprocated giving, or what I understand to be *love*.

I'm not an expert on relationships, but I believe this is how they frequently come about. And it shows that if I ever want to grow a relationship, new or preexisting, vulnerability and trust are necessary to grow authentic love.

It comes down to this:

We must take the first step.

How will you proceed, my courageous and resilient reader? I know you're resilient because this is not a disease for the faint of heart. Severely progressed, addiction is a force more debilitating than comprehension. Nevertheless, whatever you have been through, you can come out of it.

I promise.

Continuing to seek meaning in your life, in the face of suffering, is meaning enough. Open up to the possibility that support and love from your fellow brother or sister in recovery can be the strength to stay sober. A community and spiritual growth can empower you to manage your disease, and bring about true happiness, peace, and freedom in your life. This transformative experience has been the case for millions of people once afflicted as you are, if not more so. Is it not possible these opportunities are equally afforded to you, so long as you do as they did? At the very least, maybe a community, one that's suffered a similar predicament with chemicals, can provide support as you realign your actions with your values and adjust your approach to life?

It might not seem like it at first. But if you pay attention and give it enough time, you will see that everyone in recovery is on a similar trajectory. That despite personal differences and varying belief systems, a community can thrive when love and service are its guiding principles. It is the idea that we can achieve together what we will never accomplish alone—recovery from addiction, the freeing of our spirit, the realizing of our true and best self.

The best way I can describe the spiritual solution to addiction is this: there are things

I don't know; and things
I don't know I don't know.

I understand you have patiently read this book, attentive to every detail, and that your brain is possibly spinning at this point. But please, hang in there.

There are things *I don't know.*

For me, this means math. I do not care much for math. I have never been exceptionally skilled at math. Even with a patient and Zen-like math instructor, I'm unable—more likely unwilling—to grasp most concepts. I'm incredibly fortunate, as are you that being a counselor requires little in the way of mathematical ability.

Then, there are things *I don't know I don't know.*

Remember the ignorance of being a child? How wonderful to be oblivious to the world, its inhabitants, and all the needless suffering!

Your guardians are your world and ensure your security.[50] There's no worrying about war, world hunger, economic insecurity, insurance premiums, terrorism, healthcare, and the like. Life is considerably more manageable when we lack knowledge of the more terrifying aspects of existence.

The spiritual solution to addiction is something *I don't know I don't know*. By having a new spiritual experience with a Power greater than myself, I access a solution previously unimaginable. By working the Steps with a sponsor, being of service to others, we learn how to love ourselves. I know how to fill my cup, and my cup overflows. Where there was once fear and emptiness in the pit of my stomach, I now find strength, inner peace, and readiness to do the next right thing. I'm not happy all the time, but I am fundamentally okay with myself. And I am confident that if I continue operating my life in the manner first taught to me by my community all those years ago,[51] I will continue to experience life in such a beautiful and fulfilling way.

My friend, the only way to experience anything, is to act.

I plead with you to join us as we emerge from our addicted hells, walk with heads held high, bring about a new approach to life, and give thanks that recovery is possible.

With boundless love,

Joseph Caravella
Burns Ave
Saint Paul, MN 55106

June, 2019

---

[50] I'm sorry if they didn't.
[51] *Pray; clean house; help others.*

Bibliography

Inaba, D., & Cohen, W. E. (2011). *Uppers, Downers, All Arounders: Physical and Mental Effects of Psychoactive Drugs 7th ed.* Ashland, OR: CNS Publications.

Inaba, D., & Cohen, W. E. (2014). *Uppers, Downers, All Arounders: Physical and Mental Effects of Psychoactive Drugs 8th ed.* Medford, OR: CNS Publications.

White, William L. (1998). *Slaying the Dragon: The History of Addiction Treatment and Recovery in America.* Normal, IL: Chestnut Health Systems/Lighthouse Institute.

(2016). *Facing Addiction in America: The Surgeon General's Report on Alcohol, Drugs, and Health.* Rockville, MD: U.S. Department of Health and Human Services, Public Health Service, Office of the Surgeon General.

Hostetter, M., & Klein, S. (2017). *In Focus: Expanding Access to Addiction Treatment Through Primary Care.* New York, NY: The Commonwealth Fund.

Frankl, Viktor E. (1984) *Man's Search for Meaning: An Introduction to Logotherapy.* New York: Simon & Schuster.

Reyes, H. (2007). *The Worst Scars Are in the Mind: Psychological Torture.* Int Rev Red Cross 89:591–617.

Smith, P. S. (2006). *The Effects of Solitary Confinement on Prison Inmates: A Brief History and Review of the Literature.* Crim Just 34:441–568.

Abramsky S., & Fellner, J. (2003). *Ill-equipped: U.S. Prisons and Offenders with Mental Illness.* Human Rights Watch, pp. 145–68.

Kim, K., Becker-Cohen, M., & Serakos, M. (2015). *The Processing and Treatment of Mentally Ill Persons in the Criminal Justice System: A Scan of Practice and Background Analysis*. Urban Institute.

National Human Genome Research Institute. *Why Are Genetics and Genomics Important to My Health?* (FAQ, Sept. 11, 2018). Retrieved from https://www.genome.gov/19016904/faq-about-genetic-and-genomic-science/.

Diaz, K. M. et al. (2017). *Patterns of Sedentary Behavior and Mortality in U.S. Middle-Aged and Older Adults: A National Cohort Study*. Annals of Internal Medicine 167(7). DOI:10.7326/M17-0212.

American Psychiatric Association. (2013). *Diagnostic and Statistical Manual of Mental Disorders, Fifth Edition*. Arlington, VA: American Psychiatric Publishing.

Mubanga, M. et al. (2017). *Dog Ownership and the Risk of Cardiovascular Disease and Death—A Nationwide Cohort Study*. Scientific Reports 7, Article number: 15821.

Perissinotto, C. M. et al. (2012). *Loneliness in Older Persons: A Predictor of Functional Decline and Death*. Arch Internal Med. 2012;172(14):1078–84. doi:10.1001/archinternmed.2012.1993.

(2012). *Addiction Medicine: Closing the Gap between Science and Practice*. New York, NY: The National Center on Addiction and Substance Abuse at Columbia University.

Marable, M. et al. (1999). *Let Nobody Turn Us Around: Voices on Resistance, Reform, and Renewal an African American Anthology*. Lanham, MD: Rowman & Littlefield Publisher.

Wilson, Bill. (1976). *Alcoholics Anonymous: The Story of How Many Thousands of Men and Women Have Recovered from Alcoholism*. New York, NY: Alcoholics Anonymous World Services.

Merton, Thomas (1955). *No Man Is an Island*. New York, NY: Harcourt, Brace.

Dennis, M. L., Foss, M. A., & Scott, C. K. (2007). *An Eight-year Perspective on the Relationship between the Duration of Abstinence and Other Aspects of Recovery*. Evaluation Review, 31(6), 585–612.

De Soto, C. B., O'Donnel, W. E., & De Soto, J. L. (1989). *Long-term Recovery in Alcoholics*. Alcoholism: Clinical and Experimental Research 13, 693–97.

Berridge, K. C., & Robinson, T. E. (1998). *What Is the Role of Dopamine in Reward: Hedonic Impact, Reward Learning, or Incentive Salience?* Brain Research Reviews 28, 309–69.

McLellan, A. T. et al. (2000). *Drug Dependence, a Chronic Medical Illness: Implications for Treatment, Insurance, and Outcomes Evaluation*. JAMA 284 (13): 1689–95.

(2017). *National Diabetes Statistics Report: Estimates of Diabetes and Its Burden in the United States*. Atlanta, GA: U.S. Department of Health and Human Services, Centers for Disease Control and Prevention.

Di Chiara, G., & Imperato, A. (1988). *Drugs abused by humans preferentially increase synaptic dopamine concentrations in the mesolimbic system of freely moving rats*. Pro Natl Acad Sci USA, 85(14), 5274-8.doi:10.1073/pns.85.14.5274

Tomasello, M. (2014). *The Ultra-Social Animal*. European Journal of Social Psychology, 44(3), 187–94. http://doi.org/10.1002/ejsp.2015.

Retrograde Extrapolation

May 22, 2008, the night I drank myself to death and survived.

Personal information, such as weight and amount of liquor consumed, pulled from the medical record obtained from Northwestern Memorial Hospital, documenting my weekend stay in their intensive care unit, May 23-25.

163lbs x 1.0kg/2.2lbs = 74.1kg

50.721 oz. (1.5L of vodka) x 29.6mL/oz x 40mL EtOH/100mL x 0.789g/mL = 473.8g consumed

C_o = 473.8g/0.68 L/kg x 74.1kg x 10 dL/L = 0.940 g/dL

Time for elimination = 11 hours (I passed out around 2200, then admitted to the emergency room at 0900)

11 hours x 0.023% per hour (adjusted for alcoholic elimination rate) = 0.253%

Conc. Eliminated = 0.253%
C_o = 0.940%

BAC at time of passing out = 0.940% - 0.253% = 0.687[52]

0.45% is the accepted lethal dose in 50% of adult humans

My dose was 0.687%

---

[52] Amazingly, my BAC at the time of admission to the emergency room that morning was still 0.140—eleven hours after last consuming vodka.

CPSIA information can be obtained
at www.ICGtesting.com
Printed in the USA
JSHW022220230321
12836JS00004B/156